BLAZERS

The World's Deadliest

The Deadliest Jobs on Earth

by Connie Colwell Miller

Reading Consultant:
Barbara J. Fox
Reading Specialist
North Carolina State University

Content Consultant:
Jennifer A. Hess, DC, MPH, PhD
Research Associate and Ergonomist
Labor Education and Research Center
University of Oregon

CAPSTONE PRESS
a capstone imprint

Blazers is published by Capstone Press,
151 Good Counsel Drive, P.O. Box 669, Mankato, Minnesota 56002.
www.capstonepress.com

Books published by Capstone Press are manufactured with paper
containing at least 10 percent post-consumer waste.

Library of Congress Cataloging-in-Publication Data
Miller, Connie Colwell, 1976–
     The deadliest jobs on earth / by Connie Colwell Miller.
     p. cm. — (Blazers books. The world's deadliest)
     Includes bibliographical references and index.
     Summary: "Describes deadly jobs and what makes them dangerous" — Provided by publisher.
     ISBN 978-1-4296-3931-6 (library binding)
     1. Hazardous occupations — Juvenile literature. I. Title. II. Series.
HD7262.M55 2010
331.702 — dc22   2009031860

Editorial Credits
Kathryn Clay, editor; Matt Bruning, designer; Svetlana Zhurkin, media researcher;
     Laura Manthe, production specialist

Photo Credits
Alamy/Chris Cheadle, 27; Michael Doolittle, 25
DVIC/U.S. Marine Corps photo by Staff Sgt. William Greeson, 17
Getty Images/Reportage/Christopher Pillitz, 29; Stone/Tyler Stableford, 21, 23; The Image Bank/
     Chip Porter, 11
iStockphoto/sean boggs, cover (firefighter)
Photolibrary/Alaskastock, 5
Shutterstock/Andrejs Pidjass, 28 (design element); Anthony Jay D. Villalon, 13; dedaiva bg,
     12 (design element); Dole, 26 (design element); Ilja Mašík, cover (design element); Ivan
     Harisovich Khafizov, 18 (design element); Jeff Thrower, 7; Norman Chan, 15; objectsforall,
     28 (design element); Richard Sargeant, 16 (design element); Thomas Sztanek, 9; Worldpics,
     20 (design element); Yuri Bershadsky, cover (design element); Zsolt Horvath, 26
     (design element)
Thinkstock, 19

TABLE OF CONTENTS

Chapter 1
Deadly Jobs.   4

Chapter 2
Sort of Dangerous   6

Chapter 3
Very Dangerous   14

Chapter 4
Extremely Dangerous.   22

Glossary.   30

Read More.   31

Internet Sites.   31

Index.   32

DEADLY JOBS

Freezing waters. Spinning blades. Armed criminals. These are just a few dangers workers face around the world. Every day, people risk injury or death while on the job.

DEADLY FACT

Men are more likely than women to be killed at work.

Chapter 2

SORT OF DANGEROUS

TRUCK DRIVER

Truck drivers around the world face dangers on the road. Poor weather or road conditions can cause accidents. Truckers who haul dangerous chemicals are especially at risk. In a crash, trucks could explode.

DEADLY FACT

Long hours put truckers at risk of falling asleep while driving.

FARM LIFE

Farmers use powerful machines to **harvest** crops. **Combines** use sharp blades to cut crops. Other farm machines have belts and rollers. Farmers can get caught and injured in the machines.

harvest – to collect and gather crops

combine – a large farm machine that is used to gather crops

SMALL PLANE PILOT

Small plane pilots face many dangers in the air. Storms can rock small planes. Engines can fail. Flights over foggy mountains are especially dangerous and deadly.

DEADLY FACT

Rescue workers often have a hard time reaching crash victims in wooded areas.

HIGH VOLTAGE

Electrical power line workers handle dangerous wires. Workers can be burned or **electrocuted** by the large, powerful wires. They often work from great heights and risk deadly falls.

electrocute – to kill with a severe electrical shock

13

Chapter 3

VERY DANGEROUS

DEADLY SITES

Cars and trucks whiz past road construction sites at high speeds. The fast-moving vehicles can strike workers. Bulldozers, dump trucks, and cranes also cause deadly injuries.

15

MILITARY TROOPS

Military troops fight in deadly battles. They can be injured while operating heavy machinery or firing weapons. Soldiers travel in armed vehicles that can crash or be attacked.

DEADLY *FACT*

In 2008, more than 300 U.S. troops were killed in Iraq.

ARMED AND DANGEROUS

Police officers fight dangerous **criminals**. Some criminals carry hidden weapons. Traffic stops can turn into deadly high-speed car chases.

DEADLY FACT

More than 140 law enforcement officers die on the job every year.

criminal – someone who commits a crime

BURIED ALIVE

Miners crawl deep beneath the earth to dig up **minerals**. They spend long hours in small spaces without fresh air. Cave-ins trap workers underground.

mineral – a material found in nature that is not an animal or a plant

DEADLY FACT

Thousands of people die each year inside China's coal mines.

Chapter 4

EXTREMELY DANGEROUS

FIGHTING FIRES

Raging flames and blinding smoke put firefighters at risk. Forest fires cause deadly burns. Rescue workers have died from breathing in too much smoke.

IRON WORKERS

Iron workers climb tall **scaffolding** to work on buildings and bridges. High winds can cause deadly falls. Falling beams can strike workers without warning.

DEADLY FACT

Heated metal can create dangerous gases. Iron workers injure their lungs from breathing in the gases.

scaffolding – wooden or metal framework that supports workers

FOREST LOGGER

Loggers cut down trees with chainsaws and other dangerous machines. They can be struck by tree branches. Loggers may also fall from mountain slopes or treetops.

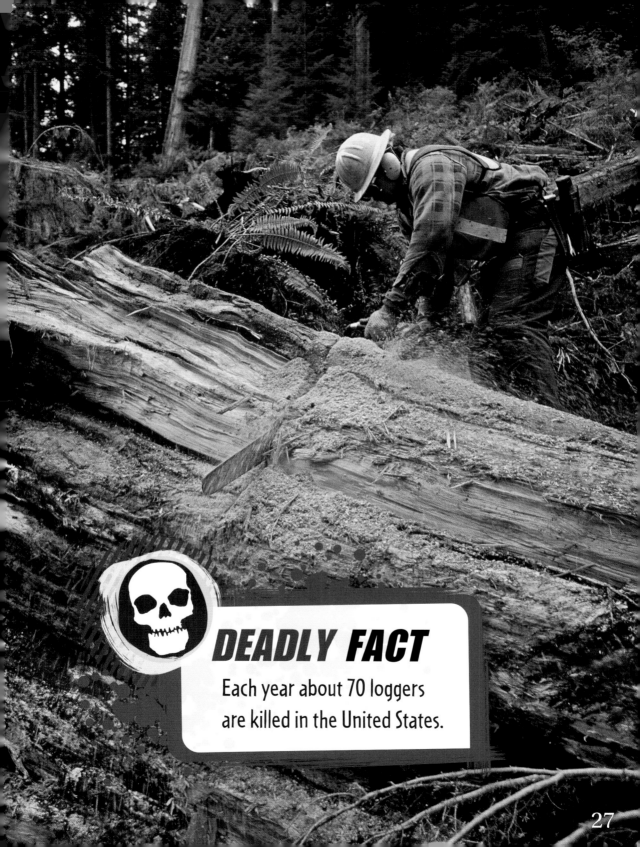

DEADLY FACT

Each year about 70 loggers are killed in the United States.

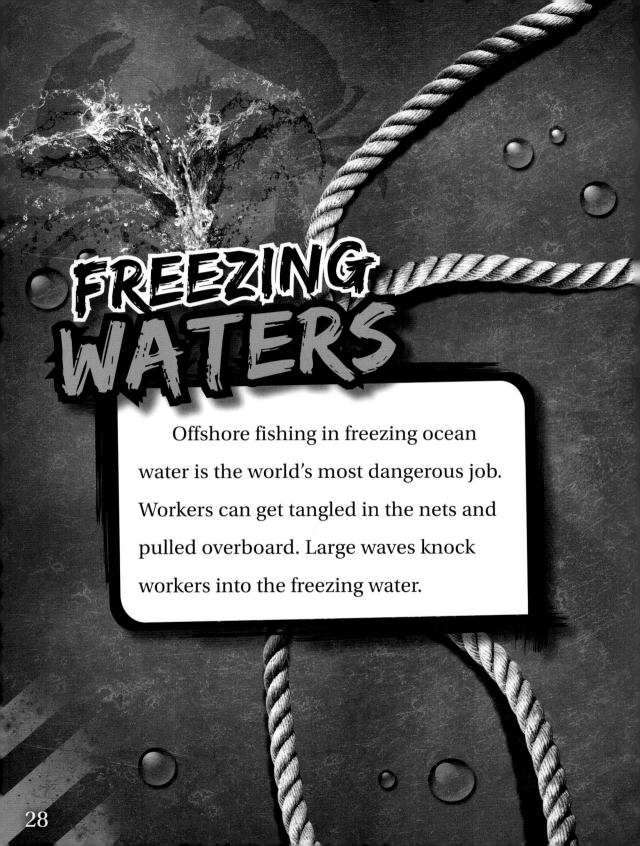

FREEZING WATERS

Offshore fishing in freezing ocean water is the world's most dangerous job. Workers can get tangled in the nets and pulled overboard. Large waves knock workers into the freezing water.

Workers brave icy waters, burning buildings, and steep heights every day. Though dangerous, the jobs they do make people's lives better.

GLOSSARY

combine (COM-byn) — a large farm machine that is used to gather crops

criminal (KRI-muh-nuhl) — someone who commits a crime

electrocute (i-LEK-truh-kyoot) — to kill with a severe electric shock

harvest (HAR-vist) — to collect and gather crops

miner (MINE-ur) — someone who digs up minerals from the ground

mineral (MIN-ur-uhl) — a material found in nature that is not an animal or a plant

scaffolding (SKAF-uhl-ding) — wooden or metal framework that supports workers

READ MORE

Gonzalez, Lissette. *Police in Action*. Dangerous Jobs. New York: PowerKids Press, 2008.

Loveless, Antony. *Fighter Pilots*. The World's Most Dangerous Jobs. New York: Crabtree, 2009.

O'Shei, Tim. *The World's Most Dangerous Jobs*. The World's Top Ten. Mankato, Minn.: Capstone Press, 2007.

INTERNET SITES

FactHound offers a safe, fun way to find Internet sites related to this book. All of the sites on FactHound have been researched by our staff.

Here's all you do:

Visit *www.facthound.com*

FactHound will fetch the best sites for you!

INDEX

airplane pilots, 10

chemicals, 6
construction workers,
    14
criminals, 4, 18

dangerous heights, 12,
    24, 26, 29
dangerous machines,
    8, 14, 16, 26

electrical power line
    workers, 12

falling objects, 24, 26
farmers, 8
firefighters, 22
freezing waters, 4,
    28, 29

iron workers, 24

loggers, 26

military, 16, 17
miners, 20, 21

offshore fishers, 28

police officers, 18

rescue workers, 10, 22

truck drivers, 6